The place we call Heaven

will one day appear

When earth is no longer

serving you here

From body to spirit
transition's a breeze
As light, love and beauty
surround you in peace

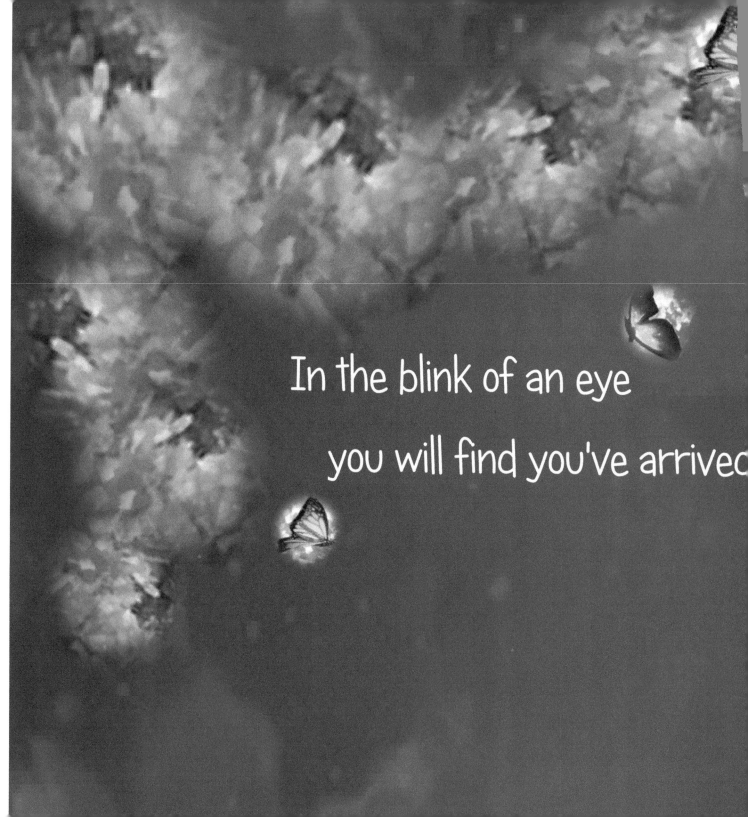

In the blink of an eye

you will find you've arrived

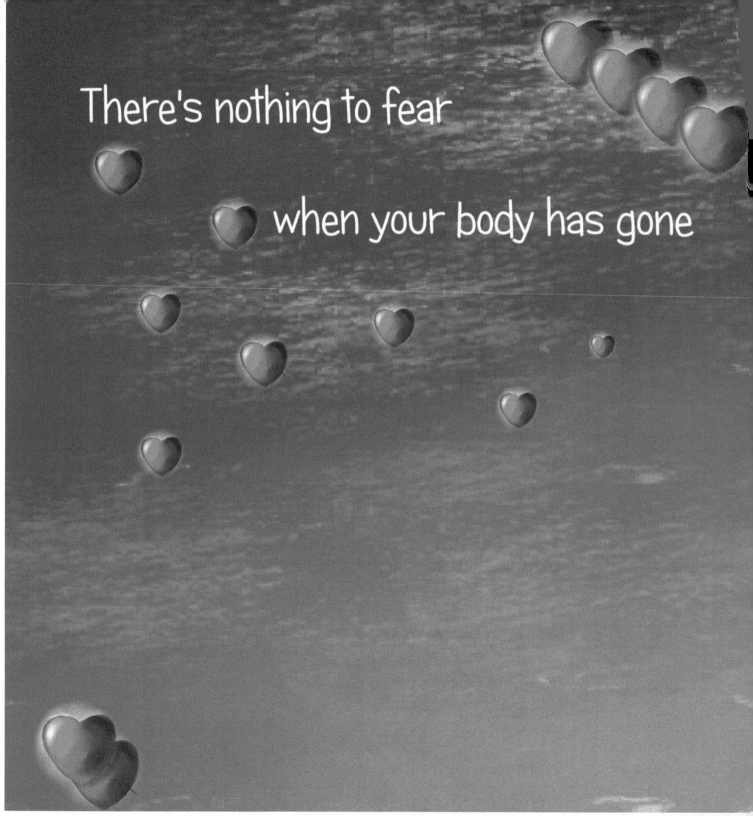

or your heart, soul and spirit

will always live on

There are people you love
and animals too
That are happy and joyful
and waiting for you

There's so much to see

you're never alone

You'll feel so excited

For this is your home

You'll create with your thoughts

and you'll see that it's true

That anything's possible

to be, have and do

You'll plan your adventures and do what you love

Explore the big
Universe
amongst
stars above

As you look all around

you know it's the place

Where you were created

in God's special space

Remember you're always

surrounded by love

Whether here on this earth

or in Heaven above

What Happens When We Die is the first of a 3 book series.
1. What Happens When We Die - published in April 2019
2. Why Are We Here - To be published in July 2019
3. Where is God - To be published in Sept 2019

About the Author

Patricia May is an author, speaker, and teacher that loves inspiring children through the books she creates, presentations she gives and classes she teaches. Patricia writes these books to answer some of the big questions children ask in a way that is positive and loving and feels good to them.

This is the first of a three book series called "Enlighten Kids." "Why are We Here," and "Where Is God" are soon to follow.

Patricia May lives in the beautiful foothills of Amador County with her husband Dave, her pups, and all her kids and grandkids living not too far away.

Please join us to keep up on all the newest books that will soon be available,

www.Patricia-May.com

blissfulkidscoaching@yahoo.com

www.factbook.com/blissfulkidscoaching

CPSIA information can be obtained
at www.ICGtesting.com
Printed in the USA
BVHW022328130222
628955BV00004B/121